# Sir Francis Drake

## *Devon's flawed hero*

## Alex White

*Bossiney Books·Launceston*

**Acknowledgements**
The illustrations are reproduced by kind permission as follows:
Mary Evans Picture Library, cover, pages 14 and 17;
Plymouth City Libraries, pages 1 and 18.
Other pictures are from the publisher's own collection.

This reprint 2010
First published 2003 by
Bossiney Books Ltd, Langore, Launceston, Cornwall PL15 8LD
www.bossineybooks.co.uk
ISBN 978-1899383-51-1
© 2003 Alex White       All rights reserved
Printed in Great Britain by R Booth Ltd, Penryn,, Cornwall

# Introduction

When Sir Francis Drake's fever-ridden corpse was lowered into the sea in 1596, he was already a figure of truly legendary status. Throughout Europe people spoke in hushed tones of the 'sea-dragon' who had single-handedly circumnavigated the globe and brought the great Spanish Empire to its knees. Of course, such tales were based more on fantasy than fact. Drake was certainly not the spotless hero of popular mythology, but neither was he the villainous pirate of Spanish folklore.

Some despised him for his stubbornness, arrogance and greed; others spoke kindly of his warmth, compassion and generosity. What then is the truth behind the legend? Who was Drake and what were his real achievements? These are some of the questions that this book seeks to answer.

## Drake's early life

Drake's incredible success is all the more remarkable in the light of his humble parentage. In an age when English society was rooted in hierarchy and privilege, Drake's birthplace was no grander than a tiny leasehold farm called Crowndale, just south of Tavistock in Devon. Though he would rise to become one of the most celebrated men of his age, Drake would never fully escape the social stigma surrounding these modest beginnings.

Drake's birth-date is unknown – probably some time between 1539 and 1542. Whatever the year, he was born into a nation still in the grip of the religious and political upheavals of the English Reformation. At the root of this turmoil was a series of laws passed by Henry VIII in the 1530s and early 1540s. Through these he had broken England's ties with Rome by establishing the Church of England and making himself its head, in place of the Pope. Henry's motives for these changes were practical: they gave him the freedom to divorce (and thus, he hoped, to ensure a smooth succession of the throne after his death) and the opportunity to raise revenue by repossessing church property and land. Otherwise, Henry had little interest in changing the nation's religious beliefs and it was only when he died in 1547 that the pace of change accelerated dramatically.

The new king was Edward VI (Henry's son by Jane Seymour), but he was still a boy and power rested with his advisors, led by the Duke of Somerset. For these men the break with Rome was more than a convenient excuse to legalise divorce and raise revenue. It was the first step in the conversion of England to a new kind of Christian faith – Protestantism – that was sweeping through western Europe at breakneck pace.

Inspired by Martin Luther and his followers, Protestants sought to replace the authority of the Church with the divine authority of the scriptures themselves. They argued that, instead of bowing and scraping before the local priest, the individual's primary obedience should be to God and their own conscience. With this new emphasis on internal truth the external trappings of the Catholic Church came to be regarded as an irrelevance. Stunned parishioners looked on as the elaborate icons and tapestries of the past were replaced with plain walls and simple wooden altars.

Such radical changes were bound to cause unrest. In Devon and Cornwall the trigger proved to be a decree issued in 1549. It stated that all churches were to adopt a new prayer book which, in line with Protestant thinking, was to be printed in English and not the traditional Latin – particularly galling for the those in the far west whose mother tongue was Cornish. It was a step too far. A makeshift army marched on Plymouth and Exeter and members of the new Protestant land-owning elite cowered in hedgerows as their properties were put to the torch. As the head of a Protestant family himself, Drake's father insisted that they left Devon for fear of religious persecution.

Recent historians have questioned whether a modest family like the Drakes would actually have been in any danger from the uprising. It has been suggested that Drake's father simply used the rebellion as a convenient excuse to flee from an allegation of horse-theft and assault. Either way, the boy Drake was uprooted and soon found himself casting off from Plymouth in a small boat bound for Kent. It was an experience that would stay with him for years to come, and it no doubt contributed to his growing hatred of the Catholic faith.

On a more positive note, Drake took his first steps into the life of the seaman. His new home was aboard a houseboat on the river Medway in Kent and, for the first time, he slept with water lapping beneath him and gulls circling above. Then, at dawn, he awoke to the sight of dozens of small cargo and fishing boats making their way out to the ocean and, more inspiring still, the mighty ships of the royal navy that dwarfed his tiny boat as he taught himself to row. Little wonder, then, that by his early teens Drake's itchy feet had carried him aboard a small merchant boat making regular trips to the Netherlands and France. He was to spend much of his adolescence aboard her and it seems that he excelled at the job: when the boat's owner died, he left the vessel to his young apprentice. But the ambitious Drake was never one to rest on his laurels. Having learnt much of the art of sailing and the hardships of the common seaman's life, he took his small boat and sailed for Plymouth and a new life of wealth and adventure on the high seas.

## A family business

When Drake returned to Devon, Plymouth was thriving – its superb natural harbour having enabled it to develop rapidly as a port and fishing centre. In addition there was the Tamar estuary and its tributary, the river Tavy, along which tin from south-west Dartmoor and cloth from Drake's home town of Tavistock could be transported into Plymouth before being shipped on to continental ports. If Drake was daunted by this bustling new scene he never showed it and his remarkable determination and ambition would soon see his career take off. He also had the immediate advantage of being related to the wealthy Plymouth ship-owner, John Hawkins.

Hawkins inherited his small fleet of merchant ships from his father who had amassed a considerable fortune trading West African ivory to the Portuguese colonies in Brazil. More recently, John Hawkins had proved that selling African slaves to Spanish colonies in the Caribbean could be equally profitable. Indeed, the family's ongoing success was a factor in allowing Plymouth to overtake Dartmouth as the main West Country port.

It is, of course, unpleasant to remember the role that slavery played in the development of Plymouth and indeed the entire Western world. How, we find ourselves asking, did rational, civilised and often deeply religious men participate in such an evil trade? Sadly, there is no room to answer that question here, except by saying that it was taken very much for granted. Whether you were Protestant, Catholic or Muslim, slavery was just an accepted fact of sixteenth century life, and it was not unknown for Devonians themselves to be captured by Arab slavers – a recent estimate is that more than a million Europeans were taken into slavery in Africa and the Middle East between 1550 and 1700.

If John Hawkins probably never thought twice about the morality of slavery, he certainly would have considered its dangers. Apart from the inevitable risks involved in all ocean travel at this time, there was the fact that Spain officially forbade any trade between her Caribbean colonies and the rest of the world. Flouting that ban was no laughing matter in an age when Spain was a major world power, with an Empire covering much of Central and South America.

The arteries of this Empire were its shipping routes, along which Spanish treasure fleets returned with cargoes of silver and gold that the English could only dream of. Anyone posing a threat to these routes posed a threat to King Philip II – King of Spain and the most powerful man in Europe. Such was the climate in which Hawkins' illegal trade was conducted and, although the corruption or carelessness of Spanish officials allowed his early voyages to go unpunished, he would not always be so lucky.

It is unclear exactly how John Hawkins was related to Drake, who was ten years his junior. It is often said that the two were simply cousins but the evidence is inconclusive. Whatever the relationship, Drake was not deterred by the risks. He soon talked John into giving him a place on his voyage of 1566-67. Although Drake held a relatively lowly rank on this voyage, he must have been delighted as he sailed out into the Atlantic for the first time. Not only was he destined for parts of the world few had ever seen, he also stood to make a tidy profit if things went well. Such thoughts of riches were certainly not beneath a young man who had seen and envied the lifestyle of his well-heeled Plymouth relatives.

Relatively little is known of Drake's part in this first trip – though we do catch an interesting glimpse of him successfully converting a Welsh shipmate to his own Protestant beliefs. In contrast, the voyage itself ended in costly failure when, as Drake saw it, the English were tricked out of ninety slaves by a dishonest Spanish official.

A disappointed young Drake returned to have his misery compounded by the news of his father's death. But things would get worse still with his next voyage aboard Hawkins' slave ships.

## Disaster at San Juan d'Ulua

They set sail again in October of 1567, with John Hawkins leading the small fleet of six ships and Drake as a junior officer aboard the flagship – the ageing *Jesus of Lubeck*. It seems Hawkins was impressed with Drake's talents, however, and he soon promoted him to captain of the *Judith* (a modest ship of around fifty tons).

After a difficult crossing of the Bay of Biscay, the fleet reached the Guinea Coast in West Africa where superior weaponry and the clever manipulation of inter-tribal feuding enabled them to capture around four hundred prisoners. With this human cargo stored in gruesome conditions beneath their feet, they made for the Caribbean and, after several profitable months of trading, were hoping for nothing more than an uneventful return to Plymouth. Unfortunately, their hopes were soon dashed when they hit a fierce storm off the Florida coast. The *Jesus of Lubeck* was so badly damaged that there were fish swimming in her hold!

Suddenly Hawkins was in desperate need of a harbour. With his flagship sinking beneath him, his only choice was the Mexican port of San Juan d'Ulua. When the fleet limped into this tiny Spanish harbour on 16 September 1568 Hawkins was delighted to find that it provided excellent shelter, but there was a catch. Spanish locals informed Hawkins that a fleet was expected within a fortnight and with it would be Don Martin Enriquez – Viceroy of Mexico and one of the most powerful men in the Spanish Empire. England and Spain would not be formally at war for another twenty years but, as the head of a band of glorified smugglers, Hawkins was still in a nasty predicament.

Until now he had been dealing with local governors, most of whom had either lacked the power or the inclination to comply with official Spanish policy, but with Don Martin Enriquez things would be different, and he knew it.

His only hope was to repair the *Jesus* as quickly as possible and make for the Atlantic before the Spanish fleet arrived. Fate dealt the English a cruel blow, however, and they awoke the next morning to

*An artist's impression of the fight at San Juan d'Ulua*

the sight of Spanish sails on the horizon. As predicted, the Spanish Viceroy was not best pleased to find a harbour filled with uninvited foreign guests and his anger grew still further when Hawkins effectively held the town to ransom – saying he would allow the Spanish to enter only if they guaranteed the safety of his fleet. Unable to anchor and in a weaker position to defend, Enriquez was forced to concede.

With the two fleets now lying side by side, Spanish and English sailors whiled away the time talking shop and even exchanging friendly banter, but Don Martin Enriquez was in a less hospitable mood. He hatched a plan to bring troops from the nearby town of Vera Cruz and, on 23 September, they launched a devastating attack in which the *Jesus* and two other English ships were lost. As the drama unfolded, fortunate positioning allowed Drake and his crew to escape to the mouth of the harbour where, together with Hawkins – who had made a narrow escape in another ship – he anchored for the night.

By morning, though, the *Judith* had mysteriously disappeared and Hawkins would later accuse Drake of deserting him. This grave charge has often been repeated by Drake's detractors; whether or not it is fair is hard to say. Perhaps Drake was right to judge that there was little more he could do and simply refused to put his crew at any further risk.

Either way, the disaster's impact on Drake was phenomenal. Not only had he seen several hundred of his countrymen killed or taken prisoner, he had also had his first small taste of wealth stripped from him. Drake was not a man to take such losses lightly. His fierce Protestantism had always made him suspicious of the Catholic Spanish, but now he was convinced he had first hand experience of their treachery and for literally decades to come this experience would focus his mind on one thing – revenge.

## A private war

Drake was not the only one brooding on the disaster at San Juan d'Ulua. A new-found hatred for Spain emerged right across the West Country as bereaved families mourned their loved ones. Meanwhile, at court, Queen Elizabeth I was under pressure from the Spanish ambassador who, rightly, suspected her of playing a part in the illegal voyage.

There was nothing particularly remarkable in this – Elizabeth had very little in the way of an official royal navy and she often invested in private ventures, hoping to profit alongside their entrepreneurial captains. The unwritten condition of such investment was that she could conceal her involvement if things went wrong and this proved unusually hard in the case of San Juan d'Ulua. As a result it came to mark an important deterioration in Anglo-Spanish relations.

In this atmosphere of growing tension, Drake travelled to London to ask permission for a reprisal voyage to the Caribbean. In truth, it was a rather naïve request at a time when the Queen and her advisors were struggling to avoid war with Europe's most powerful nation. Besides, they did not share Drake's personal thirst for vengeance and he was soon refused.

For a few months Drake paused – marrying his first wife, Mary Newman, at the parish church of St Budeaux (which is now part of

Plymouth). Little is known of Mary; although a cottage in Saltash is claimed to be her childhood home, she may have been a Londoner. Either way Drake's mind was still half a world a way and, in the next couple of years he made two further voyages to the Caribbean, neither of them with full royal consent.

Little is known about the first of these ventures but, during the second, the stocky young Drake began to make a name for himself as a skilful opportunist raider. More importantly, he caught a glimpse of the true weaknesses of the Spanish Empire which, vast though it was, was also young and thinly defended. With this realisation to boost his natural confidence, Drake's eyes now lighted on the tiny Spanish outpost of Nombre de Dios on the Panamanian coast.

For much of the year Nombre de Dios was a sleepy backwater, with little in the way of adequate fortification. Every so often, though, the town became a hive of activity, as the Spanish treasure fleet anchored to collect gold and silver arriving by mule train from the mines of Chile and Peru. With this combination of vast riches and minimal defences, Drake judged the town to be the Empire's Achilles' heel and it was his primary target when he returned to the area in 1572.

For all the vulnerability of Nombre de Dios, attacks on Spanish colonies were still comparatively rare and the plan was a bold one. Amazingly, Drake sailed with just two ships and 73 men and boys – many of whom were friends or relations of his from Plymouth and Tavistock. With such a tiny force, he knew it would be madness to attack when the treasure fleet was at anchor. Instead, his plan was to catch the town off guard by arriving before the fleet and making off with any treasure which had been stored. With this in mind he led his tiny band of men into the town early in the morning of 28 July 1572 and, by advancing confidently to the sound of trumpets and drums, they bluffed the Spanish into believing they were out-numbered.

As their bewildered enemy tried to regroup, Drake's men stumbled upon a vast pile of silver but Drake, convinced that there were even richer prizes, ordered them to leave it where it was. Then, hampered by torrential rain and increasing Spanish resistance, the attack party moved on to the town's treasure house. Just as they were set to break down its door, Drake collapsed from a leg wound he had received earlier in the night. Dispirited, his men carried him back to the boats without an ounce of treasure in their pockets and, for all its boldness and cunning, the raid ended in dismal failure.

Although Drake recovered quickly, the months that followed were miserable for him. One of his brothers was killed in an unsuccessful raid and another died from an epidemic of yellow fever that swept through the crew, leaving almost half of them dead. Only in January of the following year did things look up. At last, he got news of mule-trains bringing more treasure to Nombre de Dios.

Drake's first attempt to ambush one of these ended in another frustrating failure, when a drunk and over-enthusiastic English sailor blew their cover.

At this point Drake might have been forgiven for succumbing to the old sea-going superstition of the cursed voyage and sailing for home. But the future 'sea-dragon' was not one for turning – especially when there was booty involved. Instead he organised another ambush and, thanks in part to the help of a group of French seamen and a community of escaped slaves, his persistence finally paid off. After a daring escape, the crew at last had the treasure they had been promised and, four months later, they returned to a hero's welcome in Plymouth.

## The circumnavigation

Government officials were slower to celebrate Drake's exploits. Official relations with Spain had improved during Drake's absence and, once again, his adventures were causing political embarrassment for the Queen. Probably this led her to instruct Drake to lie low for a while and virtually nothing is known of his activities over the next two years.

When Drake does reappear, we see him contributing to the campaign in Ireland – where the English were trying to secure another foothold for Protestantism. Thoughts of Spanish treasure were never far from Drake's mind, however, and as memories of his earlier voyages began to fade Drake proposed yet another raid on King Philip's South America colonies.

Finally the Queen gave him her consent but, as a naturally cautious monarch, she was still wary of risking outright war with Spain. As a result she made no formal mention of plundering Spanish booty and Drake's written orders were simply to explore the Pacific coast of

South America in search of uncharted territory. Nonetheless it is unlikely that Elizabeth was genuinely expecting mere exploration from a man with Drake's growing reputation. She was, after all, a major backer of the voyage and, like the other investors, she was hoping for big returns. It would have been entirely in keeping with her character if she secretly instructed Drake to seek these returns as he saw fit.

This delicate political situation surrounding the voyage meant that very few of the 164-man crew were aware of their true destination when they left Plymouth in December 1577. Most of them thought they were embarking on a routine trading voyage to the Mediterranean. Unsurprisingly there was some concern when Drake led the ships off into the virtually unknown waters of the South Atlantic and, although he managed to calm some frayed nerves by capturing an experienced Portuguese navigator, tension still ran high through the long days at sea.

This unrest soon took on a peculiarly personal note for Drake when one Thomas Doughty began slowly to undermine his command. Drake had befriended Doughty in Ireland and his influence in the Court had helped him in raising the money for the current voyage. Yet, possibly through jealousy at his friend's growing success, Doughty became increasingly hostile towards Drake.

As the voyage progressed, he could be heard boasting of his influence in London, exaggerating his own importance to the current expedition and slyly questioning Drake's authority. If Doughty thought his social standing would allow him to get away with all this, he knew very little of his friend. Drake was never a man to push too far and, after a series of increasingly tense confrontations, he decided to try Doughty for mutiny.

With the ships lying at anchor off the Argentinian coast, a jury was sworn in and Drake presented Doughty with the reasonably plausible charge of mutiny and the rather less plausible one of witchcraft. Doughty was well acquainted with legal proceedings, however, and he quickly questioned the trial's legality. Where, he asked, was the formal commission from the Queen granting Drake the right to sit in judgement over such a court? It was a good question because, with all the secrecy surrounding the mission's objectives, Drake probably did not have one. Temporarily flustered, Drake claimed to have left the document in his cabin and, at that moment, Doughty must have known his fate was sealed. The jury of forty men soon returned the verdict Drake wanted and two days later, on 2 July 1578, Thomas Doughty was beheaded. Then, with a characteristic touch of theatre, Drake held his old friend's head aloft and cried 'Lo! This is what happens to traitors!'

Drake's excessively hasty and probably illegal trial of Thomas Doughty has left a permanent stain on his reputation. Yet it is easier to understand his motives if we remember that, as the commander of a small force in unknown waters, the threat of mutiny was a very real danger for him. This threat had increased dramatically when Doughty's complaints began to strike a chord with a significant minority of the crew – namely the so called 'gentlemen voyagers'.

These dozen or so men were mostly from wealthy land-owning families and had no intention of sharing the burden of the common sailor. Instead, they sat idly by as the mariners strained away before them and this had caused an underlying class conflict that was dogging the voyage. Doughty's complaints exacerbated this conflict. He gave voice to the grudges of his peers who, like him, envied and resented the command of the lowly Drake.

Of course Drake himself was not entirely free of blame. His growing arrogance and stubbornness often rubbed people up the wrong way and would lead to similar situations in the future. Nevertheless, if he was to stop the rot that had already set in, he had little choice but to make an example of his old friend.

Following the execution Drake made an uncharacteristically eloquent speech insisting that, from now on, the whole crew must work together regardless of class. With the fleet now entering the Strait of Magellan, at the tip of South America, this was more than empty rhetoric. For three hundred miles, ice-capped mountains loomed on either side as the crew battled with winds strong enough to throw whirlpools in their path. Then, after just fourteen days, they entered the Pacific.

It had been a truly remarkable piece of seamanship; without a reliable map or accurate navigational equipment, Drake had passed through the unknown Strait in what was probably the fastest time that century.

Unfortunately there was no time to celebrate. Almost immediately, Drake's ships were hit by a devastating storm and for days they fought for survival as its power drove them relentlessly south. For the twenty-nine men of the *Marigold*, it was all too much. Their screams rang out through the fog as she went down with the loss of all hands. Shortly afterwards the *Elizabeth* was separated from Drake's *Golden Hind* and, either at the will of her captain or of her exhausted crew, she passed back through the Strait and returned to Devon.

It was only after more than fifty days of abysmal weather that the storm clouds finally cleared, leaving Drake and the crew of the *Golden Hind* alone in a vast and unknown ocean.

There followed an important geographical discovery. For decades there had been speculation about the existence of a continent below South America, the so-called *Terra Australis*. Now the storm had driven the *Golden Hind* far enough south for Drake to learn that, if it existed at all, it must be elsewhere. This was something of a mixed blessing, since the discovery of another continent as rich in resources as South America would have been a major triumph for the English.

For Drake, though, it was probably a relief to know that he could forget about exploration and turn his mind to looting instead. After all, he may have been isolated behind enemy lines but he had one crucial advantage – nobody knew he was there.

Recognising this, Drake turned north on what was to become a devastating voyage of plunder. It got off to a bad start, when natives ambushed and killed two of his crew, but things soon picked up when Drake's men overwhelmed the small Chilean town of Valparaiso without a shot being fired. Then, having stowed their prizes including four chests of gold, they continued northwards, plundering as they went from whatever small boats and settlements they could find. Previously complacent Spanish officials were shocked by 'the boldness of this low man' and panic began to spread through the Empire. The worst was yet to come, however, for Drake now hunted down and caught an important Spanish treasure ship nicknamed the *Cacafuego*. After a brief skirmish, the English boarded her to find that she was fully laden with gold, silver and jewels estimated to be worth more than half the

*Opposite: A contemporary print showing a European, probably Drake, being greeted by Native Americans on the west coast of North America*

annual revenue of the English crown. At that instant, every member of Drake's crew knew they were rich beyond their dreams – if they could just get home.

So far the Spanish had been caught off guard but Drake knew it could not last. He sailed north, hoping to escape them via the sea passage that was believed to exist round the top of North America but, when he rightly began to suspect that the passage was a myth, he turned back and paused to restock on the Californian coast. Now he had two distinctly uninviting options – continue round the world or return the way he had come. If he retraced his steps it would mean facing the newly alerted Spanish and the chance of further storms. If he continued, he would have to take his priceless cargo through the South Pacific and Indian Oceans, of which he knew nothing except that they were filled with potentially hostile Portuguese ships.

It was a big risk but Drake judged that continuing was the lesser of two evils and, on 23 July 1579, the *Golden Hind* embarked on its long journey across the Pacific.

Sixty-eight gruelling days later, Drake's exhausted crew finally reached the Philippines. After a small clash with the natives, they managed to restock before sailing on to the Moluccas where, through peaceful trading, they were able to fill the *Golden Hind's* remaining space with valuable ginger, cloves and pepper. With this out of the way, Drake proved his formidable seamanship yet again by crossing the Indian Ocean, rounding South Africa and bringing the *Golden Hind* safely home to Plymouth on 26 September 1580.

It was not the first circumnavigation of the globe – that prize had gone to Magellan's crew some sixty years before (though Magellan himself was killed by natives in the Philippines). Yet the fact that Drake's men were so often alone in unknown and hostile waters makes his voyage an unsurpassed achievement, even in the great age of discovery.

For all the brilliance of Drake's seamanship, however, his future still hung in the balance as he entered the familiar waters around Plymouth. If the Protestant Elizabeth was still on the throne he was confident of a hero's welcome but, if she had been succeeded by the Catholic Mary Queen of Scots, he was more likely to face some pretty indisputable charges of piracy. Desperate to know their fate, the

*Another print from Dirk ('Theodorus') de Bry's* Americae, *showing Drake in the East Indies*

*Golden Hind's* sunburnt crew held their breath as Drake asked a local fisherman if the Queen was still alive. To their great relief, he confirmed that she was.

## Our Golden Knight

Needless to say, Drake's investors were delighted with all this and they rubbed their hands in smug anticipation of their vast returns. King Philip, on the other hand, was less amused and promptly demanded that all the stolen treasure should be returned to Spain. Once again, the Queen was faced with a delicate political situation of Drake's making. Yet the sheer extent of Drake's booty, and a day spent being

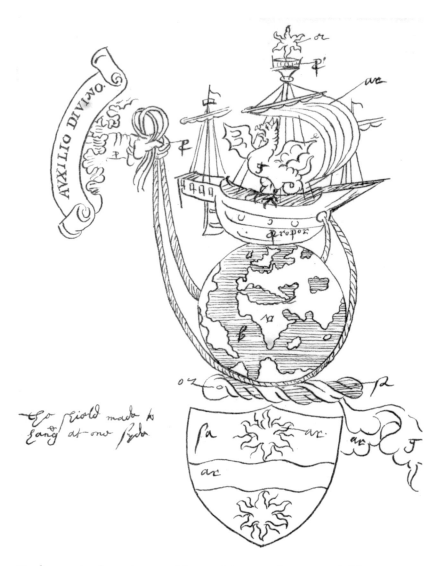

Drake spent a long time working on his coat of arms, and this was what he came up with. The note says 'The shield made to hang at one syde.' The emblematic ship has circumnavigated the world 'auxilio divino', by the help of God – and God's hand can be seen holding two helpful tow-ropes enthralled by his heroic tales, was enough to persuade Elizabeth to take a calculated risk and keep the treasure. She judged that this alone would not make Philip declare war since he was already fighting in the Netherlands and faced another possible war in France. Luckily, the gamble paid off. Most of the treasure was hidden in the Tower of London and for two years both she and Drake all but denied its existence. Eventually the Spanish complaints died down, though the bitterness remained.

In the mean time Drake began to socialise with the elite of English society and, while many still considered him a vulgar upstart, he bought the support of others through his lavish generosity. It proved easier to win the affections of the Queen herself and Drake soon became something of a royal favourite – with Elizabeth once calling for him nine times in a single day!

The icing on this royal cake came in April 1581, when a vast crowd saw him knighted on the deck of the *Golden Hind* at Deptford. With this Drake became the most famous man in England. Never having been particularly modest, he revelled in his fame and bragged of his achievements to anyone who would listen. Even the long suffering Spanish Ambassador was subjected to an earful of his boasting! But Drake was also now one of the richest men in England. Knowing that words alone could not seal his reputation, he set about acquiring all the trappings of the true Elizabethan gentleman. He sat for portraits, worried about his new coat of arms and began to invest heavily in property – most of it in the West Country.

For his new home Drake chose Buckland Abbey, just a few miles south of his home town of Tavistock. This stunning property (now managed by the National Trust and open to the public) was originally constructed as a Cistercian monastery in the thirteenth century. Like so many others, it passed into private hands during the turmoil of the Reformation and, when Drake took control of the Abbey and its five hundred acres of grounds in December 1580, it was in the possession of Richard Grenville, an old rival of Drake's for the Queen's favour. Grenville had poured his heart into improving the Buckland estate and only let it go when Drake offered the then princely sum of £3500.

At such a price the Abbey became an important status symbol for Drake but, not satisfied with this alone, he also bought manors at

Yarcombe (near Honiton) and Sampford Spiney (near Tavistock) as well as buying enough Plymouth shops, houses and taverns to make him the town's second biggest private landlord. On top of all this, the Queen granted Drake several estates – including Sherford manor near Plymouth – and, though some of these gifts proved to be of little worth, they all added to the aura of respectability that Drake was keen to create.

He was further assisted in this by being elected Lord Mayor of Plymouth in 1581. As such he soon proved himself to be an excellent local administrator with a particular interest in law and order. Indeed, Drake remained a justice in the town long after his year as Mayor was over and he ploughed substantial amounts of his own money into the town gaol.

Drake also entered Parliament around this time, becoming MP for Bossiney (in the parish of Tintagel in North Cornwall) in October 1584 – an opportunity he owed largely to the influence of Francis Russell, Earl of Bedford, who had become his godfather while his family had rented their small Crowndale farm from his father nearly half a century before. Over the years, Russell had developed an admiration for his godson who was, like himself, a devoted and patriotic Puritan. It was his efforts which secured Drake's Bossiney seat.

When Drake returned to London his services were much in demand. He sat on endless committees, most of which probably bored the old sea-dog to tears. Only when talk turned to corruption in the navy, the preservation of Plymouth harbour, or the establishment of English colonies in North America can we imagine Drake paying full attention. It is no great surprise then that, when his term ended in 1585, Drake made little effort to keep his Bossiney seat. Yet his time in parliament had been far from wasted. With his natural enthusiasm, Drake made friends as easily as enemies and now those friends included some of the most powerful men in England. Many of them would be vital allies in the future.

In the midst of his public triumphs, Drake faced private tragedy when Mary died in the bitter winter of 1583 and was buried at St Budeaux church, where they had been married less than fourteen years before. It had been a curious marriage – Mary had spent most of it waiting to hear if her husband was alive or dead and there is very little to tell us whether either of them was truly happy. Drake remarried two years later – and in stark contrast to Mary, his new wife was from a well-connected aristocratic family. Her name was Elizabeth Sydenham – daughter and heiress of Sir George Sydenham, Sheriff of Somerset, and one of the richest men in the West Country. With this impressive match, Drake's place in English society was, at last, on firm ground.

## Raiding the West Indies

While Drake was busying himself with politics and social climbing, Spanish pressure on England was growing. For a start Philip had virtually doubled the size of his empire by forcibly pressing home his claim to the Portuguese crown in the autumn of 1580. Then there was the conflict in the Netherlands where Protestant Dutch rebels were resisting the Spanish presence. Elizabeth had been supporting these rebels for years but in 1584 they suffered serious defeats and suddenly it seemed that Spain might at last secure a base for an invasion of England.

The following year Philip seized numerous English merchant ships. When Elizabeth retaliated by encouraging English reprisals, war began to look inevitable.

In this frosty political climate, the Queen was persuaded to launch a pre-emptive attack on Philip's Caribbean ports. Drake was, of course, the only man for the job. On 14 September 1585 he sailed out of Plymouth at the head of some 33 vessels and over 2000 men. Sir Francis was justifiably proud of this impressive fleet, which was by far the largest he had ever commanded, and he could not resist flexing his muscles on the Spanish coast. Landing at the Spanish port of Vigo, he raided parts of the town, burnt a chapel and stole some supplies before heading for the Caribbean and his first major target – Santo Domingo, on the island of Hispaniola.

Santo Domingo was an impressive town with good defences, but the Spanish had failed to protect one crucial flank adequately – thinking that three miles of dense jungle would be defence enough. This understandable oversight allowed Christopher Carleill (the brilliantly talented leader of the English ground forces) to march 800 men straight into the heart of the city. Over the next few days, the

Englishmen systematically ransacked the town and, as was usual on Drake's voyages, they demonstrated their Protestant convictions by desecrating religious artefacts.

In the course of all this looting, there was a nasty incident when Drake's black messenger boy was murdered under a flag of truce. In retaliation, Drake killed two Spanish friars and vowed that he would do so every day until the murderer was executed – which he was, the following day. This chilling little episode certainly displays Drake's capacity for cruelty. Yet it also reflects a regard for the lives of non-whites that often marked Drake out from his contemporaries. Above all, it highlights Drake's growing frustration with the process of agreeing a ransom price for the town of Santo Domingo. When he arrived, Drake had hoped to set this price at some 500,000 ducats but, after extensive negotiations, he was forced to accept the humiliating sum of just 25,000.

In the wake of this disappointment Drake set his sights on the mainland town of Cartagena where, once again, the efforts of Carleill ensured that the raid was a staggering military success. Financially, though, it proved almost as disappointing as that on Santo Domingo and morale plummeted. To make things worse, the fleet was now suffering from a fever that had killed upwards of 300 men and it was soon painfully clear to all, including Drake, that they had no choice but to cut their losses and sail for home.

It had been an expensive venture. Drake had not even covered his costs, despite losing upwards of 750 men – so much for curbing the wealth of the mighty Spanish Empire! But the majority of Englishmen remained ignorant of these failings and heralded the voyage as a resounding success. Military heroics were celebrated, costs were forgotten, and a wave of patriotism swept the country. The legend of Drake was fast being born.

## The coming of war

When Philip heard that Drake was up to his old tricks again he was livid. He committed himself to an invasion of England knowing that, if he was successful, he would cut Elizabeth's support for the Dutch rebels and so kill two Protestant birds with one stone.

Out of context this plan might seem like a piece of inexcusable imperialism. Yet it is worth remembering that Philip actually had a claim to the English crown because, as the husband of Elizabeth's immediate predecessor, Mary Tudor, he had briefly been King of England. Equally importantly, Philip enjoyed the support of millions of Catholics across Europe, who believed he was embarking on a legitimate holy war to support Rome and preserve the sanctity of the one true faith.

Back in England, Elizabeth was also burning her bridges and committing to war. In February 1587, she finally executed Mary Queen of Scots for plotting against her life. Then, in March, she gave Drake orders to disrupt Philip's invasion plans as he saw fit – including by direct attacks on Spanish towns. The following month, he sailed for the southern Spanish port of Cadiz with a fleet of 23 ships.

When Drake arrived in Cadiz, on 19 April, he found the harbour filled with around 60 Spanish ships and, without pausing to regroup or outline a proper plan of attack, he sailed on in. This apparently reckless move infuriated at least one of his more cautious officers, but it also caught the Spanish by surprise and, while they panicked, Drake enjoyed the run of the harbour. Then, when the townspeople rallied themselves at dawn, a freshening wind allowed the English fleet to escape – showing great seamanship in the process. The extent of the destruction they left behind is uncertain. Drake claimed that 39 ships were captured or destroyed, but Spanish sources put the figure at 25. Whatever the true figure, the raid was an astounding English success and it certainly disrupted Philip's invasion plans.

With this victory under his belt Drake's confidence soared. Undaunted by a failed attack on the town of Lagos, he soon secured Sagres harbour as a safe base for his fleet. From there, he destroyed as many as 47 small cargo boats carrying supplies essential to the Armada's preparations. Then, suddenly, he abandoned his effective blockade of the Spanish coast and sailed out into the Atlantic in search of a richly laden Portuguese cargo ship – capturing her on 9 June. When Drake returned to Plymouth later in the month, her cargo of spices, silk and jewels was valued at an incredible £108,000 – nearly thirty times what Drake had paid for Buckland Abbey.

This was, unquestionably, a shameless piece of looting, but criticism of it is unfair. By this stage the cold war that had existed between

Spain and England for two decades was all but at an end; with more than half the Elizabethan navy's funding coming from private sources, England's defences were dependent on precisely this sort of opportunism. What is more, Drake's detour led the Spanish on a wild goose chase that cost them time and money and it was this mistake, as much as Drake's activities on the Spanish coast, that caused Philip to postpone his invasion for a valuable extra year.

## The Armada

Drake's reaction to his victories on the Spanish coast was uncharacteristically modest. Instead of boasting, he urged caution and stressed the extent of Spanish sea power that remained untouched. In fact, Philip's preparations were in a state of crisis. His men were badly hit by typhus and had little to eat but rotting provisions. Meanwhile he was overworking himself and was at one point bed-ridden for a month. He put so much pressure on the Armada's commander, the Marquis of Santa Cruz, that he too fell ill and eventually died in February 1588.

Philip replaced him with the Duke of Medina Sidonia – a curious decision since the Duke had little combat experience and even less self-belief. Indeed, Medina Sidonia thought the whole project was doomed to failure and he even asked to be excused on the grounds of his acute seasickness! His one saving grace as commander was that he was a superbly efficient administrator and, by April 1588, the invasion preparations were back on track.

In England, Drake's lowly birth prevented him from taking supreme command of the fleet – that post went to the Lord Admiral, Lord Thomas Howard, with Drake being made Vice-Admiral. Like Medina Sidonia, Howard had little combat experience, but fortunately he was far less pessimistic than his Spanish counterpart and had the additional advantage of being an excellent listener. Throughout the campaign he showed himself willing to learn from Drake's experience and soon established a good working relationship with him (no easy task, as Doughty and others like him had found to their cost). Most importantly, however, Howard was a nobleman and, as such, would find it far easier to command the respect of his captains than a self-made man like Drake.

The early spring of 1588 found Drake worrying about a plan to divide the English fleet between the east and west ends of the Channel. This seriously flawed strategy was supported by both Howard and the Privy Council and, had it been adopted, events might have been very different.

Fortunately it was not. Drake and common sense prevailed and the fleet was united at Plymouth on 23 May 1588. With this obstacle out of the way, Drake, who had long believed that the Spanish were most vulnerable when anchored on their own coastline, was desperate to attack. He had been pushing for preliminary attacks for the past eight months, but the Queen's hesitancy and the division of the fleet had delayed him. Now, to his great frustration, he was delayed still further by unfavourable winds and a lack of provisions.

In fact, the 151 ships and nearly 30,000 men of the Armada had already set sail on 18 May. Unfortunately for Medina Sidonia, they were scattered by a fierce storm off the north coast of Spain and by the third week of June his forces were in disarray. When Drake and Howard heard this encouraging news they were keen to capitalise on the Duke's misfortune and, with the winds finally in their favour, they sailed out of Plymouth on 24 June. In the fortnight that followed, however, they were unable to engage the Armada and returned disappointedly to Plymouth. There was nothing they could do now but wait.

By the time the regrouped Armada was finally sighted off the Cornish coast on 19 July, all of England was on edge. Flaming beacons carried the news from hilltop to hilltop and dozens of makeshift armies stood at arms. In reality, though, everyone knew that bands of untrained civilians would prove no match for the professional and well-equipped Spanish army waiting in the Netherlands. If the Armada could successfully transport this army across the Channel, the result would be a formality.

Legend, of course, has Drake calmly playing a game of bowls at this pivotal moment in English history but sadly there is no contemporary evidence to support the story. In reality, with all the pressure on the navy, Drake was probably as apprehensive as anyone. At some two miles across, the Armada was certainly a sight to make even a legend tremble and, to make things worse, the English found themselves downwind of Medina Sidonia's stately procession – a difficult position in any naval battle and one that put them well and truly on the defensive.

The manoeuvre that reversed this ominous situation was one of the deftest in naval history. Under the cover of darkness, and possibly on the instruction of Drake himself, the majority of the fleet crossed directly in front of the Spanish before beating to windward of them on their southern flank. Thus at daybreak on 21 July the Spanish were stunned to find English ships chasing them down the channel in perfect formation! From this superior position Howard proceeded to harass the Spanish with cannon fire for much of the day.

As darkness fell, Drake was given the responsibility of leading the English fleet by lighting a signal beacon in his stern. Mysteriously, though, this was soon extinguished and puzzled English captains struggled to maintain their positions and wondered what had become of their elusive Vice-Admiral.

It has often been alleged that, ever the privateer, Drake put out the light in order to hunt down a richly laden Spanish ship called the *Rosario*. In fact there is little to support this accusation except the jealous testimony of another English captain and recent research has been more forgiving. It suggests that Drake spotted some lights to the south of the fleet and, thinking that they might be Spanish ships manoeuvring to a better position, went to investigate. By this account it was only after Drake had discovered the lights to be harmless German cargo ships that he captured the badly damaged *Rosario*. Either way, Drake's characteristically impetuous decision was not what was called for with stakes this high and he certainly put the fleet at some risk. Fortunately they managed to regroup at dawn.

Over the following week the English continued to hound the Armada up the channel, with major battles being fought off Plymouth, Portland Bill and the Isle of Wight. In each case, Lord Admiral Howard maintained a safe distance from the Armada and relied on his superior firepower to do what damage he could. In this way he prevented Medina Sidonia from playing the Armada's strongest card – its soldiers. Traditionally naval battles had consisted of bulky troop-carrying vessels closing each other down quickly before a bloody hand-to-hand battle was fought on deck. Spanish

*The fireships approach the doomed Armada*

ships with their oars, high stern castles, and masses of soldiers were still ideally suited to this type of battle but, over some fifty years, English ships had evolved to fight a more flexible form of warfare. Partly on the advice of both John Hawkins and Drake himself, oars had been replaced with additional cannons and stern castles shrank dramatically as a sleeker English design began to emerge. The end product was a faster, more manoeuvrable and better armed fleet and this winning combination would prevent the Spanish from fully engaging a single English ship throughout the whole campaign.

This all left Medina Sidonia in a terrible predicament as he anchored at Gravelines, near Calais, on 27 July. With the English fleet still intact, there was little hope of successfully transporting the Spanish army across the channel – especially since there were only a handful of shallow-bottomed boats to get them out to the ships in the first place. To their credit, both Medina Sidonia and the Duke of Parma (the leader of ground forces in the Netherlands) had foreseen these potential problems, but Philip's impatience and over-confidence led to them being ignored. He was about to pay for his mistake.

Just before midnight on Sunday 28 July the English launched eight fire-ships towards the Spanish position and, as the wind and tide carried these unstoppable weapons towards them, the Spanish panicked. Desperate crews cut their anchor cables, ships ran aground and there were numerous collisions in the haste to escape. Encouraged by all this confusion, Drake led the other English captains as they moved in for the kill. Now, more than ever, superior English artillery and training began to pay off as cannons blazed through the night.

By sunrise many of Medina Sidonia's ships had been seriously damaged and, with the wind turning to the south-west, they were driven out into the North Sea. With this any chance of meeting up with Parma's army quickly vanished and the Spanish now pinned their hopes on an arduous escape round the north coast of Scotland.

As they moved further north some English ships briefly gave chase but, short of ammunition and supplies, they soon gave up. In any case, the Scottish and Irish coasts were to prove far more devastating than any cannons and, over the following months, shipwrecks and unfriendly local receptions would account for some sixty Spanish ships and their crews.

## Dom Antonio's dream

As a jubilant English nation thanked God and Sir Francis Drake for their victory, the remains of the Armada lay in tatters on the north coast of Spain. Recognising that there would be no better opportunity than this to deal the Spanish a knock-out blow, Drake persuaded the Queen to support an attempt to wipe out Spain's remaining forces. It was an ambitious idea – especially since Drake was also planning an attack on Lisbon, through which he hoped to depose Philip and place one Dom Antonio on the Portuguese throne instead.

The middle-aged Dom Antonio was a curious figure and his claim to the Portuguese crown was highly questionable. Nevertheless, he had gained some favour in the English court and Drake in particular thought his quest to replace Philip in Portugal was feasible. He was wrong. It was actually a hare-brained and utterly unworkable plan because, contrary to his own deluded opinion, Dom Antonio had no popular support in either Portugal or Spain. Without that support, he posed no realistic threat to Philip.

Despite this, Drake's reputation left him little difficulty in mustering some ten thousand volunteers. Many of them were drawn by the prospect of playing a part in the final destruction of the mighty Spanish Empire. They were in for a rude awakening.

From the start, poor supplies and disease plagued the voyage and, although vastly superior forces led to the sacking of the Spanish towns of La Coruña and Vigo, bad winds and poor planning made the attack on Lisbon a humiliating military fiasco. When the scattered English fleet finally returned, more than half the soldiers and seamen were dead, but Drake and England had gained virtually nothing.

Drake was not entirely to blame for all this suffering – chance and the mistakes of others both played their parts. Nonetheless, he returned to face the wrath of Elizabeth and the Privy Council. Why, they demanded, had he focused on land attacks rather than on the final destruction of the Spanish navy as instructed? And had his own hesitation made the attack on Lisbon such a shambles? They were serious questions and it was only by dint of Drake's service record and some neatly fudged answers that he avoided punishment.

## The Plymouth leat

Perhaps Drake's most celebrated achievement of this time was the construction of the Plymouth leat, which brought fresh water to Plymouth from a point on the river Meavy some ten miles away. Like so many of Drake's accomplishments, however, there is evidence that its construction had at least as much to do with Drake's personal ambition as with his sense of philanthropy.

Contrary to popular perception, Plymouth already had a relatively good supply of drinking water from local wells and springs; had this been the only reason for the leat it would probably never have been built. A far more pressing concern was finding water for the old town mill at Millbay – which Drake had recently leased.

The mill was tidal and had been under threat as sea-levels dropped throughout the second half of the century. Back in 1584 a committee, which included Drake himself, was formed to draft a bill presenting the idea of the leat to Parliament.

The bill stressed the potential benefits, claiming that the leat would provide water for merchant shipping and fire-fighting, as well as having significant environmental benefits for Dartmoor and Sutton harbour. The subject of the old town mill was discreetly underplayed.

The bill had its first reading in December 1584. Early the following year it was forwarded to another committee for more amendments and recommendations. With characteristic guile, Drake got himself a seat on that committee also, and promptly added another clause authorising the construction of further mills on the banks of the seven foot wide waterway. Royal Assent came through in March – but was followed by a five year pause as Drake and the nation devoted their attention to the war with Spain.

When work finally began in 1590 the Mayor of Plymouth allocated £300 of privately donated money to the project and appointed Drake to oversee the leat's construction. Exactly what the project cost is a matter of some debate, but it appears that Drake made a healthy profit on the job – pocketing around £140 of this original sum. Those most directly affected by Drake's creative accounting were the landowners whom he had been trusted to compensate – many claimed to have received little or nothing from him.

The leat was completed in April 1591. Cashing in on his amendment to the original bill, Drake opened six new mills on its banks. This was a step too far for many local tradesmen, tinners and mill-owners who presented their own bill to Parliament, protesting that Drake's leat diverted so much water from the Meavy and Plym rivers that they were losing a staggering £6000 a year. They might also have added that none of the promised benefits of the leat had come to fruition. Still, it probably wouldn't have made any difference, since the committee that reviewed the bill included none other than the ubiquitous Sir Francis Drake himself. Predictably, it was soon rejected!

## A watery grave

True to form, Drake soon tired of the quiet life and by 1592 he and John Hawkins were seeking permission for yet another Caribbean voyage. The original plan for this venture was deceptively simple. They would capture the strategically important city of Panama, thus putting a stranglehold on gold exports whilst gaining a base for raids on surrounding towns. What this overlooked, however, was the extent to which things had changed since Drake's Caribbean heyday. Twenty years on, the once vulnerable towns now boasted formidable fortifications and well-armed populations. Against such defences even Drake's impressive force of six large royal galleons and 21 armed merchantmen would need to catch the Spanish off guard, but they failed to do so at virtually every turn.

For a start, financing and logistical problems prevented them from sailing until August 1595. Then, when they sailed, the aggressive Drake and more cautious Hawkins rarely saw eye to eye and, in a venture where speed was vital, the tension between them only lowered morale and caused further delays.

Worse still, they both made costly personal errors: Drake led a disastrous and poorly planned raid on the Canary Islands, while Hawkins failed to stop some Spanish frigates carrying news of their attack. They compounded these errors by anchoring in Guadeloupe and wasting far too much time preparing their attack on the Puerto Rican town of San Juan.

After these mistakes, there could be no hope of surprise when the English fleet eventually anchored near the town. Indeed, the people of San Juan had been preparing frantically for an entire week and had mustered an army of nearly 11,000 men. Faced with such a force, Drake's chances were slim and, after three days fighting and the loss of 400 men, he was forced to retreat with Spanish taunts ringing in his ears. As if this was not bad enough, a fever began to spread through the fleet, leaving John Hawkins dead and morale sinking fast. In the following months, Drake managed to salvage some pride with victories in his old stomping grounds of Rio de la Hacha and Nombre de Dios but, in reality, he still had little to show for his efforts and his main target – Panama city – remained untouched.

When Drake did at last send an army to march on Panama, the jungle proved as forbidding as any Spanish defences and exhausted English troops found themselves waist deep in mud, with disintegrating boots and inadequate rations. On top of that, the relentless rain made much of their gunpowder useless so that a relatively small Spanish force was able to turn them back before they even came close to Panama itself.

With this defeat the last realistic chance of accomplishing the voyage's objectives was gone and, as disease and despair gradually took their toll, Drake sank into deeper and deeper bouts of nostalgia and depression. Less than four weeks later, on 28 January 1596, he died from dysentery and was buried at sea.

## Closing thoughts

It is said that, an hour before his death, Drake struggled deliriously to his feet and called for his armour, in the hope that he might die a soldier, but he was too weak to stand and soon collapsed. Perhaps better than anything else, this tragic last effort illustrates the gulf between the man – mortal and flawed – and the legend, eternal and heroic.

This is not to say that Drake was never a great and inspiring leader of men. At times, he certainly was. Yet, like so many of his age, he was also a complex individual and his sometimes dazzling talents were tempered by some very human weaknesses. As an observant Spanish official once put it: 'He commands and governs imperiously. He is feared and obeyed by his men. He punishes resolutely. Sharp, restless, well-spoken, inclined to liberality and to ambition, vainglorious, boastful, not very cruel.'

And it is not just to the less appealing sides of Drake's personality that legend has been kind – his more questionable actions also tend to get glossed over. For instance, how often do we hear of his possible desertion at San Juan d'Ulua, of the bloody end of Thomas Doughty or of his failed voyages in later life?

It seems, then, that man and legend are not so hard to peel apart, but does that make the legend worthless? The answer must be no – for the real truth of Drake's legend lies not in the man, but in the English nation. When Drake was born England was still little more than an insignificant provincial backwater. When he died, it had transformed itself into a respected European power. In this, the England of Shakespeare, art flourished, a mood of independence abounded and, though few would have guessed it, the seeds were being sown for an Empire the likes of which even King Philip never imagined. As a man, Drake's contribution to this Golden Age was certainly significant. But, as a legend, he would become the very embodiment of England's new-found confidence.